SACRAMENTO KINGS

BY DAVID J. CLARKE

SportsZone

An Imprint of Abdo Publishing
abdobooks.com

abdobooks.com

Published by Abdo Publishing, a division of ABDO, PO Box 398166, Minneapolis, Minnesota 55439. Copyright © 2023 by Abdo Consulting Group, Inc. International copyrights reserved in all countries. No part of this book may be reproduced in any form without written permission from the publisher. SportsZone™ is a trademark and logo of Abdo Publishing.

Printed in China.
052022
092022

Cover Photo: Ezra Shaw/Getty Images Sport/Getty Images
Interior Photos: Melinda Nagy/Shutterstock Images, 1; Robert Sullivan/AFP/Getty Images, 4, 8, 31; Jed Jacobsohn/Getty Images Sport/Getty Images, 7, 10; Mark J. Terrill/AP Images, 9; Bettmann/Getty Images, 12, 40; Focus on Sport/Getty Images, 15, 24; Focus on Sport/Getty Images Sport/Getty Images, 17, 29, 38; Steve Yeater/AP Images, 19, 21; Lachlan Cunningham/Getty Images Sport/Getty Images, 22; AP Images, 27, 36; Gerald Herbert/AP Images, 32; Ron Schwane/AP Images, 33; Hy Peskin/Getty Images, 34; Vince Bucci/AFP/Getty Images, 39

Editor: Charlie Beattie
Series Designer: Joshua Olson

Library of Congress Control Number: 2021951676

Publisher's Cataloging-in-Publication Data

Names: Clarke, David J., author.
Title: Sacramento Kings / by David J. Clarke
Description: Minneapolis, Minnesota : Abdo Publishing, 2023 | Series: Inside the NBA | Includes online resources and index.
Identifiers: ISBN 9781532198434 (lib. bdg.) | ISBN 9781098272081 (ebook)
Subjects: LCSH: Sacramento Kings (Basketball team)--Juvenile literature. | Basketball--Juvenile literature. | Professional sports--Juvenile literature. | Sports franchises--Juvenile literature.
Classification: DDC 796.32364--dc23

TABLE OF CONTENTS

CHAPTER ONE

BIBBY'S BIG SHOT 4

CHAPTER TWO

THE KINGS GO WEST 12

CHAPTER THREE

WEARING THE CROWN 24

CHAPTER FOUR

ROYAL MOMENTS 34

TIMELINE 42

TEAM FACTS 44

TEAM TRIVIA 45

GLOSSARY 46

MORE INFORMATION 47

ONLINE RESOURCES 47

INDEX 48

ABOUT THE AUTHOR 48

BIBBY
10

BIBBY'S BIG SHOT

In the 2002 National Basketball Association (NBA) playoffs, the two best teams played in California. That was about all they had in common.

The defending champion Los Angeles Lakers were flashy, fitting their glamorous city. Movie stars watched on from the stands. The Lakers had megastars of their own in center Shaquille O'Neal and shooting guard Kobe Bryant. Their coach was NBA legend Phil Jackson, who had already won eight titles.

The other great team came from the northern part of the state. Sacramento was known as the home of just two things—California's state capital and the NBA's Kings. The Sacramento Kings were the opposite of Los Angeles's style on the court. They had skilled players but no superstars. They were a gritty team that shared the ball. They ran an offense that relied on teamwork and constant movement.

The Kings built the NBA's best record during the 2001–02 season with a collection of solid veteran players.

They were also incredibly good. With a 61–21 record, the Kings had more wins than any other NBA team during the 2001–02 season. Even the Lakers trailed them at 58–24. Everyone expected a showdown between the two teams in the Western Conference finals. And that's exactly what happened.

THE REAL FINALS

The New Jersey Nets were waiting for the winner in the NBA Finals. But many people thought the real championship was the Western Conference finals between Sacramento and Los Angeles. Most league experts thought whoever won this series would defeat New Jersey.

More Cowbell

Lakers coach Phil Jackson added fuel to the rivalry with an infamous quote during the 2002 playoffs. He tried to insult Sacramento by calling it "an old cow town." During the next game, Sacramento fans brought cowbells to ring. It created a Sacramento tradition that still stands.

For the Lakers that would mean another title in their notable history. But Sacramento had never won. The Kings were an original NBA team. They had been playing since 1946. But Sacramento was the fourth city that they had called home. The franchise had won the NBA Finals once, in 1951. That was 34 years before the team ever played in Sacramento.

Guard Mike Bibby, *right*, and forwards Peja Stojaković, *left*, and Chris Webber, *center*, were the Kings' three leading scorers during the 2001–02 season.

Smart drafting and trading by general manager Geoff Petrie had started to build a winning Kings team by 2000. Now Sacramento was ready to win it all. And the Kings were hungry to get one over the mighty Lakers.

BUZZER BEATER

The series was tight from the start. The teams alternated wins through the first four games. Then Game 5 in Sacramento came down to the wire. The Kings trailed 91–88 with one minute to go. It was now or never.

Sacramento got a break when Bryant fouled Mike Bibby. The Kings' point guard strolled to the line and drilled two free throws. Now it was a one-point game.

Mike Bibby puts up his winning jumper against the Los Angeles Lakers in Game 5 of the 2002 Western Conference finals.

Bryant tried to get past Kings center Vlade Divac on the next possession, but the 7-foot Divac blocked his shot. It fell to Bibby. The Kings now had a chance to take the lead. That was easier said than done. The smothering Lakers defense did everything they could to keep Sacramento from getting an open shot. With 11 seconds left, star Kings forward Chris Webber appeared to lose the ball in the corner. However, the officials said it went out off of the Lakers.

With another chance, the Kings called timeout to set up a play. Coach Rick Adelman had Bibby pass the ball in. He sent it to Webber, then sprinted toward his teammate to get the ball back. Webber handed the ball to Bibby. In the same motion, Webber set a screen that flattened Bibby's defender. The point guard was all alone for a long jump shot. Bibby drilled it, sending Sacramento's ARCO Arena into the loudest cheer of the series.

Bibby, *right*, jumps into the arms of Kings reserve Mateen Cleaves after Bibby's decisive shot.

The game wasn't over, though. Now the Lakers called timeout. Jackson drew up a play for Bryant to take on a defender one-on-one. Bobby Jackson took on the challenge. The Kings' guard stuck to Bryant like glue, forcing the Lakers' star into a tough shot. The ball clanked off the rim as time expired. The Kings had won 92–91. They now led the series 3–2.

Kings center Vlade Divac argues with the officials during Sacramento's controversial Game 6 of the 2002 Western Conference finals.

A DEVASTATING LOSS

The Lakers had won the previous two NBA titles. They weren't going down without a fight. In another heated contest in Game 6, the Lakers held on for a 106–102 victory. Along the way they shot an incredible 27 free throws in the fourth quarter. For many Kings fans, and others who cover the league, something seemed fishy about the Lakers getting to the line that much in one quarter.

Some believed the NBA had conspired against the Kings to make sure the series went to seven games. That way the league could make more money from televising the extra contest. Others believed the NBA did not want the Kings in the NBA Finals at all. Los Angeles, the bigger and more famous city, would likely draw more TV viewers, which was better for the NBA. Both theories would explain why the referees kept making calls that benefited the Lakers.

Complaining about calls is nothing new for pro sports fans. However, both theories gained even more traction in 2007.

That year former NBA official Tim Donaghy was arrested for illegally betting on NBA games. He testified that he had given inside information to gamblers during his career. Donaghy did not work the controversial Game 6. But he later claimed the NBA had instructed the officials who did to call more fouls on the Kings. A year later NBA commissioner David Stern strongly denied Donaghy's claims. Nothing Donaghy said was ever proven to be true.

But that did not take the sting of the loss away from Kings fans. The result stung even more when the Lakers won 112–106 in Game 7 to eliminate Sacramento. Bibby's game-winner was the high point for the best Kings team in history. They have not been that close to a championship since. The memories of the 2001–02 season in Sacramento are of how one of the league's best-ever teams was somehow denied a title.

Big Shot Rob

Had Game 4 ended differently, Mike Bibby's Game 5 winner might have ended the series. The Kings had led 99–97 in Game 4 with 11 seconds left. Those 11 seconds packed in a lot of action. The Lakers' Kobe Bryant missed a potential tying jump shot. O'Neal tried to tip the rebound in. That missed too. With time running out, Kings center Vlade Divac tried to tap the ball away from the rim and kill the last few seconds. Unfortunately, it went straight to Lakers forward Robert Horry at the three-point line. He had earned the nickname "Big Shot Rob" for his clutch play in the past. And now Horry was wide open. He drilled his shot just before time expired to even the series.

CHAPTER TWO

THE KINGS GO WEST

The history of the Sacramento Kings began far away from the California capital. In the late 1940s, American professional basketball had two leagues. The National Basketball League (NBL) was formed in 1937. Nine years later, a rival league, the Basketball Association of America (BAA), began play.

Brothers Lester "Les" and Jack Harrison had a long history with basketball in Rochester, New York. In 1945 they added to it when they founded an NBL team there called the Royals.

To grab players, the Harrisons looked to the military. World War II (1939–1945) was just ending. Several men who had served in the war had been college basketball stars. The Harrisons were able to sign several players out of the military ranks, including future star Bob Davies. The Royals had enough talent to win the NBL in the team's first season.

Rochester Royals forward Maurice Stokes, *left*, and center Bob Burrow, *right*, battle for a rebound against the Fort Wayne Pistons.

After three seasons in the NBL, the Royals jumped leagues to the BAA. They took their NBL success with them, winning 45 games their first year. One year later, the two leagues merged and formed the NBA.

The Royals were one of the new league's best teams. In 1951 they proved it against the New York Knicks in the NBA Finals. Rochester jumped out to a 3–0 lead in the series, but they nearly threw it away. The Knicks charged back to win the next three. Rochester forward Arnie Risen's Game 7 double-double saved the day. Rochester won 79–75 to claim its first NBA title.

The Royals never reached those heights again, despite several more winning seasons. But by the 1954–55 season, the team began to struggle. Rochester finished 29–43 in Lester Harrison's last season as coach.

The bigger problem was the growth of the NBA. By the mid-1950s, larger cities were dominating the league. Rochester couldn't keep up. With the team losing money, the NBA asked the Harrisons to either sell the team or move.

Oscar Robertson's, *right*, arrival in Cincinnati revived the team after several losing seasons in the late 1950s.

THE CINCINNATI YEARS

The Royals found a big city home in 1957—Cincinnati, Ohio. They arrived with a young, talented roster. Jack Twyman was already a star forward when the team moved. But the arrival of guard Oscar Robertson in 1960 made Cincinnati a frequent winner.

The team had no trouble making the playoffs. It was a different story once the Royals reached the postseason. The NBA had two divisions in the 1960s. Cincinnati began the decade in the Western Division, where the dominant team

Even though the Royals/Kings were new to Kansas City and Omaha as a full-time team, local fans were familiar with them. While the Cincinnati Royals were playing games all over Ohio, they also played several in Omaha. The team traveled to Nebraska to play 12 games during a three-year stretch from 1968–69 through 1970–71.

was the Los Angeles Lakers. But in 1962–63 the Royals moved to the East. An even bigger powerhouse, the Boston Celtics, ruled there. The Royals made the playoffs every year through the 1966–67 season. But they never reached the NBA Finals.

When Cincinnati stopped making the playoffs, many fans disappeared. The Royals started playing games all over Ohio in an attempt to win over new supporters. But with fewer games in the city, Cincinnati natives grew frustrated. To make matters worse, the team traded Robertson to the Milwaukee Bucks in 1970.

MEET ME IN KANSAS CITY

Royals fans watched as their former star guard won the NBA title with the Bucks in 1971. A year later, they watched the team leave. The latest move took them to a pair of new homes. Starting in the 1972–73 season, the Royals split their time between Kansas City, Missouri, and Omaha, Nebraska.

The only problem with the move was the team's nickname. Kansas City's Major League Baseball team was already called

Kansas City Kings forward Scott Wedman lunges to block a shot against the Washington Bullets in 1978.

the Royals. To avoid confusion, the basketball team changed its name to the Kings.

Even with stars such as point guard Nate "Tiny" Archibald on the roster, the Kings were rarely successful in Kansas City. Other than a surprise run to the Western Conference finals in 1981, the Kings usually watched the postseason from home.

Just as in Rochester and Cincinnati, the Kings struggled to attract fans in their two new homes. After three years they stopped playing games in Omaha. Now they were known as simply the Kansas City Kings. But fans still didn't show up. In fact, the team's best crowds came when they played across the state in St. Louis.

SACTOWN BOUND

By the 1984–85 season, the Kings' owners had once again started looking for a new home. For the third time in the team's history, the Kings were moving west, to Sacramento, California.

While the fans in California's capital showed up from day one, they didn't see many wins. Sacramento reached the playoffs in 1985–86, its first season on the West Coast. The team didn't make it back for a decade.

It was not until the late 1990s that the Kings started to put the pieces together. The team hired Geoff Petrie in 1994 as president of basketball operations. Petrie drafted slick-shooting forward Peja Stojaković in 1996 and power forward Hedo Türkoğlu in 2000. He also made smart trades for versatile star forward Chris Webber, defensive stopper Doug Christie, and steady guard Mike Bibby. Veteran center Vlade Divac signed as a free agent.

Petrie also hired Rick Adelman as head coach in 1998. It was the final piece of the puzzle for a team that was ready to break out. The Kings reached the playoffs in eight straight seasons under Adelman.

Sharpshooter Peja Stojaković made three All-Star teams during his eight seasons in Sacramento.

The Kings racked up record win totals. After finishing a franchise-best 55–27 in 2000–01, Sacramento improved even more. The next year the Kings held the NBA's best record. Their showdown with the Los Angeles Lakers in that year's Western Conference finals produced a thrilling and controversial series. The Kings eventually fell in seven games.

That proved to be the team's high-water mark. The next
year they were knocked out of the playoffs by the Dallas
Mavericks in the second round. But that defeat came with
an even bigger loss. Webber was the team's best all-around
player. He injured his knee in the series and missed most of the
next year.

THE DECLINE

The Kings were competitive even without Webber and hoped
to contend once he returned. But they again were dumped out
of the playoffs in the second round. The best team in Kings
history began to age, and the wins disappeared. After they
lost to the San Antonio Spurs in the 2006 playoffs, the team
decided not to renew Adelman's contract.

Petrie remained in charge of the team through the 2012–13
season, but he could not repeat his success building a winner.
While he drafted players who went on to become solid players,
like Tyreke Evans and DeMarcus Cousins, the Kings continued a
streak of losing records.

Even worse, rumors began that the team might move once
again. After the 2010–11 season, it looked sure to happen. The
team had been owned by the Maloof family since 1999. But
after years of losing money, they asked the NBA for permission
to move the team once again. They also tried to sell the team
to groups who would relocate the Kings for a fourth time.

Kings forward Tyreke Evans was the 2010 NBA Rookie of the Year.

Kings forward Tristan Thompson throws down a dunk during a 2021 game against the Orlando Magic.

Possible destinations of Virginia Beach, Virginia; Anaheim, California; and Seattle, Washington, were proposed.

In the end, the Kings stayed when a group headed by Vivek Ranadivé bought the team and kept it in Sacramento. The software executive also worked toward building a new arena.

After several years of worrying that Sacramento would lose its only professional team, fans now knew the Kings were staying. A new arena, the Golden 1 Center, was completed in time for the 2016–17 season.

The only thing missing was a playoff team. The Kings churned through young players and coaches looking for the combination that would return them to the postseason.

CHAPTER THREE

WEARING THE CROWN

Before he was the Rochester Royals' first NBA coach, Les Harrison was a legendary amateur player in the city. During the 1920s he helped organize two major amateur teams in the upstate New York area: the Seagrams and the Ebers. Twenty years later, when his brother Jack founded the Rochester Pros, Les joined the team as head coach. Despite the name, the Pros were initially just a semipro team. That changed when they joined the NBL in 1945 under the new name, the Royals.

As coach, Les Harrison led the Royals to the NBL title during the 1945–46 season. Five years later, his team was playing for another championship, this time in the newly formed NBA. And Harrison had a loaded team on his bench.

The 1950–51 Rochester Royals featured four players who would eventually end up in the Basketball Hall of Fame. Point guard Bob Davies and shooting guard Bobby Wanzer

Cincinnati Royals guard Oscar Robertson, *right*, makes a move around K. C. Jones of the Boston Celtics during a game in 1964.

formed one of the NBA's most potent backcourt duos. Both were signed out of the armed forces by Harrison after World War II. Wanzer eventually replaced Harrison as the team's head coach.

The champion Royals also counted on the inside scoring of forward Arnie Risen. At 6 feet, 9 inches tall, he was one of the NBA's best early big men. Risen was the team's best scorer during the 1951 Finals against the New York Knicks. He poured in 21.7 points per game in the seven-game series.

CINCY SHARPSHOOTERS

A new set of stars formed the core of the team by the time the Royals relocated to Cincinnati in 1957. Jack Twyman was one of the first two NBA players to average more than 30 points per game over the course of a season. His 1959–60 average was 31.2. Philadelphia Warriors center Wilt Chamberlain also averaged over 30 points per game that year, finishing at 37.6.

Bobby Wanzer was inducted into the Naismith Basketball Hall of Fame in 1987.

Twyman was a product of the University of Cincinnati, which had a powerhouse basketball program. At the time, NBA teams tried to grab as many local stars as possible to help build fan support. The league even used a "territorial" draft system to steer these players to their local teams. A team could give up its first-round pick in the regular NBA Draft to instead take whichever local player it wanted.

The Royals did not use a territorial pick on Twyman. But they did use the system four times before it was abolished in 1966. They plucked Hall of Fame forward Jerry Lucas from Ohio State University in 1962. He won the Rookie of the Year Award while playing for the Royals. A year later the Royals took another Cincinnati Bearcat, forward Tom Thacker. In 1964 they added center George Wilson, also from the University of Cincinnati.

However, the best territorial pick the Royals used came before Lucas, Thacker, and Wilson. Guard Oscar Robertson came out of the University of Cincinnati in 1960. He was college basketball's all-time leading scorer when he left school. He had also led the US basketball team to a gold medal at the 1960 Olympic Games in Rome, Italy. The Royals snapped him up right away. He showed why in his first NBA game. The versatile guard scored 21 points while adding 12 rebounds and 10 assists in a win over the Los Angeles Lakers. It was the first in a career filled with triple-doubles. In his rookie year he just missed averaging a triple-double for the season.

The next season, in 1961–62, Robertson accomplished the amazing feat. His final averages were 30.8 points, 12.5 rebounds, and 11.4 assists. He was the first player to ever average a triple-double over an entire season. Robertson never did it again for a full season, though he came close. In 1963–64 he averaged 31.4 points and 11.0 assists. But his 9.9 rebounds per game was just short. No NBA player averaged a triple-double again until guard Russell Westbrook did it for the Oklahoma City Thunder in 2016–17.

Despite Robertson's success, the Royals never won a championship during his time in Cincinnati. Near the end of the 1960s, the Royals hired former Boston Celtics legend Bob Cousy as head coach. Robertson and Cousy did not get along, and the point guard was traded. By the time the team moved to Kansas City, Robertson was a Milwaukee Buck.

Nate "Tiny" Archibald fires off a pass while playing for the Kansas City Kings.

SAM AND TINY

The Kings' first superstar in Kansas City was also a point guard. Nate "Tiny" Archibald learned his basketball skills on the outdoor courts of the Bronx. He played with a playground flair that both filled baskets and wowed fans. The team's first season in Kansas City/Omaha was also Archibald's best. He led the NBA in scoring and assists and was named All-NBA for the first time in his career. Archibald's No. 1 jersey is one of 11 retired by the franchise.

If Archibald missed a shot, center Sam Lacey was likely to grab the rebound. The pair were both drafted in 1970 and played together until Archibald left the Kings after the 1975–76 season. Lacey stayed until 1981, long enough to grab a record 9,687 rebounds in a Royals/Kings jersey.

Sacramento did not get its first superstar until shooting guard Mitch Richmond joined the team before the 1991–92 season. Richmond reached the postseason only once in Sacramento. In fact, he never played on a Kings team with a winning record. But that did not stop the sharpshooter from ranking among the NBA's elite players. From 1992–93 through his final Kings season in 1997–98, Richmond was an All-Star every year.

THE REIGNING KINGS

Richmond might have helped the Kings even more by leaving the team. Sacramento sent him to the Washington Wizards in 1998 for forward Chris Webber. It was one of the first moves team executive Geoff Petrie made to eventually create the Kings' dominant 2001–02 squad.

Webber was an electrifying forward. At 6 feet, 9 inches and 245 pounds, he was strong enough to mix it up in the post. But he could also handle the ball smoothly and make any shot. Webber became the focal point of Sacramento's title challengers.

Joining Webber inside was crafty center Vlade Divac. The 7-foot Serbian was not a traditional shot blocker, but he was skilled at drawing charges. Divac was also a superb passer for a big man, which fit Sacramento's offense perfectly.

Outside, the Kings had one of the top sharpshooters in the NBA. Small forward Peja Stojaković was playing in Greece when the team drafted him in 1996. The Croatian stayed there for two years and spent two more coming off the Kings bench after arriving in the NBA. By the 2001–02 season, he was an All-Star.

Chris Webber's (4) versatility made him a great fit for the dominant Kings teams of the early 2000s.

In 1999 Sacramento drafted point guard Jason Williams. In his three seasons with the team, he was one of the NBA's must-see players. His collection of behind-the-back and no-look passes made him an instant legend. But Petrie and coach Rick Adelman didn't think his style was a good fit for the team. In the summer of 2001, they traded him to the Vancouver Grizzlies for Mike Bibby, another point guard.

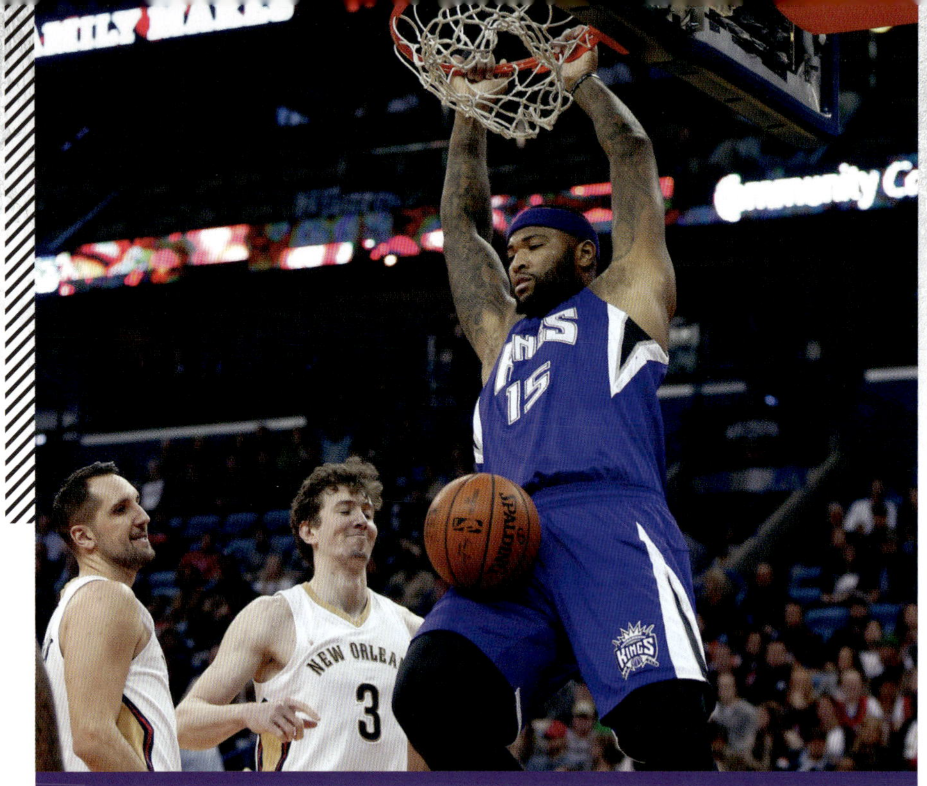

Powerful center DeMarcus Cousins (15) averaged a double-double over the course of his seven seasons with Sacramento.

Bibby wasn't nearly as flashy as Williams, but he was tough and steady. He led Sacramento to its best record ever in 2001–02. And his jumper in Game 5 of the Western Conference finals was the high point of the season.

MODERN STARS

After the Kings' golden age faded in the late 2000s, they looked for new stars. The 2009 and 2010 drafts offered promising options. Center DeMarcus Cousins was Sacramento's top pick in 2010. His 6-foot-10-inch, 270-pound frame was made for mixing it up in the NBA. He also mixed it up with officials a little too often. Despite stellar offensive numbers,

Cousins's knack for picking up technical fouls was one of the reasons he was traded to the New Orleans Pelicans in February 2017.

One of the players who came to Sacramento in the Cousins trade was small forward Tyreke Evans. It was a homecoming for him. The Kings originally drafted Evans fourth overall in 2009. Evans averaged 20 points, five rebounds, and five assists while earning Rookie of the Year honors. The only other players to ever post those rookie numbers were NBA legends Robertson, Michael Jordan, and LeBron James. But Evans slowly declined and was traded away after the 2012–13 season. His second stint with Sacramento lasted only 14 games.

Sacramento guard De'Aaron Fox (5) averaged 25.2 points and 7.2 assists during the 2020–21 season.

The Kings found their next star at the 2017 draft. Sacramento took high-scoring guard De'Aaron Fox fifth overall. In February 2022 the Kings were in the mix for a postseason spot. They swung a trade with the Indiana Pacers to add 25-year-old big man Domantas Sabonis. Kings fans hoped their team finally had the right combination of players to end nearly two decades of playoff frustration.

TIME OUT
NEW YORK
11
9
NEW
15
4
10

CHAPTER FOUR

ROYAL MOMENTS

The Rochester Royals were suddenly in big trouble during the 1951 NBA Finals. They looked to be running away with the title after defeating the New York Knicks in the first three games of the best-of-seven series. Arnie Risen had been dominant, with a double-double in each win.

However, the Knicks fought back in the cross-state series. They won three straight to send it to seven games. The final game was in Rochester. The 6-foot-9-inch Risen once again put in a towering performance. He finished with 24 points and 13 rebounds. Both totals were game highs in a 79–75 win that gave the Royals/Kings their first NBA championship.

JACK AND MAURICE

In 1958 Cincinnati Royals forward Maurice Stokes was already a three-time All-Star. The power forward was a good scorer

Royals forward Jack Twyman takes a shot against the New York Knicks in 1955.

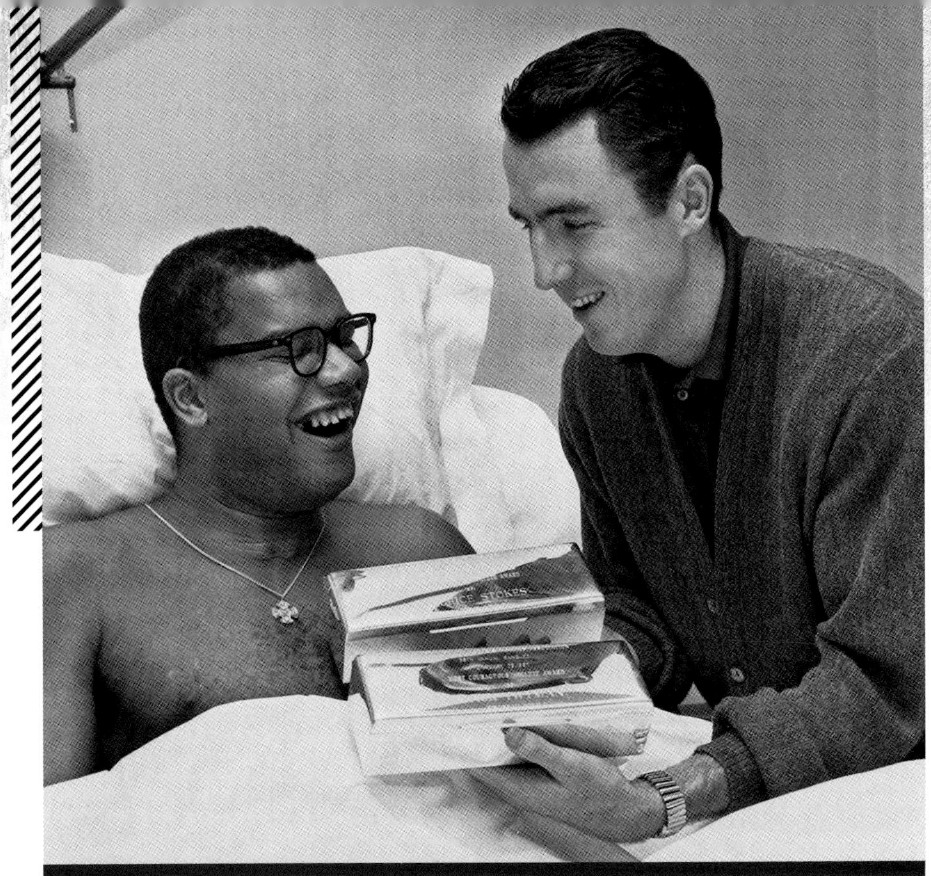

Twyman, *right*, visits teammate Maurice Stokes in the hospital after Stokes was paralyzed following an on-court injury.

and one of the league's best rebounders. But on the last day of the 1957–58 season, he was knocked unconscious making a move to the basket. At the time, concussions were treated very differently in sports. Stokes returned to the game.

The Royals had made the playoffs, and Stokes put up a double-double three days later in the opener against the Detroit Pistons. As the team was flying back to Cincinnati from Detroit, Stokes became ill on the plane. He later slipped into a coma. Stokes never recovered. A brain injury called post-traumatic encephalopathy left him paralyzed. He was also unable to speak. The once muscular power forward was no longer able to care for himself.

One of his best friends on the team had been fellow forward Jack Twyman. Now Twyman did something truly remarkable. Players at the time were not paid big salaries, so Stokes was not able to cover his medical costs. Twyman raised the money. He eventually became Stokes's legal guardian and cared for him until Stokes's death in 1970.

Three years later, the two players' story was made into a movie, *Maurie*. And in 2013 the NBA created the Twyman-Stokes Teammate of the Year Award. The award has been given out annually ever since.

CINDERELLA RUN

Playoff success was always hard to come by for the Royals/Kings, no matter where they called home. But in 1981 the team went on a surprise run. After finishing the regular season under .500 at 40–42, the Kansas City Kings didn't look like a playoff contender. Their outlook seemed even worse without injured point guard Phil Ford.

Kings coach Cotton Fitzsimmons tried a new strategy in the playoffs. He moved Ernie Grunfeld from shooting guard to point guard. The Kings also tried to slow games down. The plan worked, as the Kings beat the Portland Trail Blazers in the first round. It was the first playoff series victory for the team

Kings guard Otis Birdsong averaged a career-high 24.6 points per game during the 1980–81 season.

since 1964. Kansas City
followed that up with a
seven-game upset of the
favored Phoenix Suns. The
team reached the Western
Conference finals for the
first time since 1964 and
the last time until 2002.

MITCH CONQUERS PHOENIX

Kings fans in Sacramento
have often had to find
excitement in smaller
moments. One came

Kings guard Mitch Richmond holds up the All-Star Game MVP trophy in 1995.

when star Mitch Richmond went to the All-Star Game in 1995.
The contest featured NBA legends like Hakeem Olajuwon,
Shaquille O'Neal, and Charles Barkley. But it was Sacramento's
representative who stole the show.

After coming off the bench late in the first quarter,
Richmond lit up the scoreboard. He hit 10 of his 13 shots,
including all three of his three-point shots. At the end of
the game, he had a game-high 23 points as the Western

Oscar Robertson, *right*, is the only player in Kings franchise history to ever win an NBA MVP Award.

Conference won 139–112. Sacramento's shooting guard left Phoenix's America West Arena as the game's MVP.

THE MAYOR

One of the Kings' greatest heroes was an NBA player who never played a single game for them. Kevin Johnson was a point guard for the Cleveland Cavaliers and Phoenix Suns during his 13-year NBA career. After retiring in 2000, he went into politics. By 2011 he was the mayor of Sacramento.

Having an NBA player in the mayor's office was a huge benefit for a city that wanted to keep its team. Johnson worked tirelessly to help the Maloof family find a buyer that would keep the team in town. That ultimately led to the sale of the team to Vivek Ranadivé and the building of the Golden 1 Center. After two major moves in franchise history, and then years of uncertainty in Sacramento, the team finally had a stable home in California's capital for years to come.

Avoiding a Rare Collapse

How rare would the collapse have been had Rochester lost the 1951 NBA Finals? In the league's history, no team has ever lost a seven-game series after winning the first three games. In fact, only two other teams have ever forced a seventh game after being down 3–0—the 1994 Denver Nuggets and the 2003 Portland Trail Blazers.

TIMELINE

1945

The Rochester Royals join the National Basketball League. They capture the league title in their first season.

1948

The Royals leave the NBL for the Basketball Association of America. A year later the leagues merge to form the modern NBA.

1951

Arnie Risen's double-double in Game 7 of the NBA Finals defeats the New York Knicks and earns the Royals their first NBA title.

1957

The Harrison brothers move the Royals to Cincinnati.

1958

Maurice Stokes is injured in the team's regular-season finale. Three days later he suffers a seizure on the team plane and is paralyzed.

1961

Royals guard Oscar Robertson wins the NBA Rookie of the Year Award after averaging 30.5 points, 10.1 rebounds, and 9.7 assists during the regular season.

1962

Robertson becomes the first player to average a triple-double over the course of an entire season. The Royals reach the playoffs for the first time since the 1957–58 season.

1972

The team relocates to Kansas City, Missouri, and Omaha, Nebraska, and is renamed the Kings. In its first season, guard Nate "Tiny" Archibald becomes the first player to lead the NBA in scoring and assists in the same year.

1981

The Kings finish 40–42 but win their first two playoff series since 1964 before falling to the Houston Rockets in the Western Conference finals.

1985

The Kings move once again, this time to Sacramento. They reach the playoffs in their first season in California but lose in the first round.

1994

Former Portland Trail Blazers guard Geoff Petrie is named the Kings' president of basketball operations.

1998

The Maloof family buys a minority stake in the Kings. They take over majority ownership in 1999.

2002

The Kings finish with the NBA's best record of 61–21. They reach the Western Conference finals before falling to the Los Angeles Lakers in a controversial seven-game series.

2013

The Kings narrowly avoid moving again when the Maloofs sell the team to software company executive Vivek Ranadivé.

2016

Construction on the Golden 1 Center is completed, ensuring the Kings' future in Sacramento.

FRANCHISE HISTORY
Rochester Royals (1945–57)
Cincinnati Royals (1957–72)
Kansas City–Omaha Kings
(1972–75)
Kansas City Kings (1975–85)
Sacramento Kings (1985–)

NBA CHAMPIONSHIPS
1951

KEY PLAYERS
Nate Archibald (1970–76)
Mike Bibby (2001–08)
Bob Davies (1948–55)
De'Aaron Fox (2017–)
Jerry Lucas (1963–69)
Mitch Richmond (1991–98)
Arnie Risen (1948–55)
Oscar Robertson (1960–70)
Peja Stojaković (1998–06)
Maurice Stokes (1955–58)
Jack Twyman (1955–66)
Bobby Wanzer (1948–57)
Chris Webber (1998–2005)

KEY COACHES
Rick Adelman (1998–2006)
Lester Harrison (1948–55)

HOME ARENAS
Edgerton Park Sports Arena
(1948–55)
Rochester Community War
Memorial (1955–57)
Cincinnati Gardens (1957–72)
Municipal Auditorium
(1972–74, 1978–79)
Omaha Civic Auditorium
(1972–77)
Kemper Arena (1974–79,
1980–85)
ARCO Arena I (1985–88)
Sleep Train Arena (1988–2016)
Known as:
ARCO Arena II (1988–2011)
Power Balance Pavilion
(2011–12)
Golden 1 Center (2016–)

TEAM
TRIVIA

FILLING IT UP

Jack Twyman holds the team record for points in one game. He scored 59 in a 122–118 victory over the Minneapolis Lakers on January 15, 1960.

ROAD WOES

During the 1990–91 season, the Kings had a respectable 24–17 record at ARCO Arena. But they finished 1–40 away from Sacramento. The Kings' only road win came November 20, 1990, an 87–82 victory at the Washington Bullets. No NBA team has ever had a worse road record.

SWEET SOUNDS

Sacramento Kings forward Wayman Tisdale was also an accomplished jazz musician. Tisdale spent six seasons with the Kings from 1989–1994 as part of a 12-year career. He also released eight jazz albums before his death in 2009.

DOUBLE CALL TO THE HALL

Cincinnati Royals stars Oscar Robertson and Jerry Lucas were both inducted into the Basketball Hall of Fame twice: once for their careers in the NBA and also as members of the US men's basketball team that won the Olympic gold medal in 1960.

GLOSSARY

assist
A pass that leads directly to a basket.

clutch
An important or pressure-packed situation.

conspire
Secretly work together, often in an illegal way.

double-double
Accumulating 10 or more of two certain statistics in a game.

foul
Illegal contact with another player during the course of the game.

franchise
A sports organization, including the top-level team and all minor league affiliates.

guardian
A caretaker for another person who is not physically, mentally, or legally able to care for themselves.

post
The area around the basket where power forwards and centers usually play.

screen
When an offensive player legally blocks the path of a defender to create space for a teammate to shoot or pass.

semipro
A team where players are paid, but not enough to earn a living.

triple-double
Accumulating 10 or more of three certain statistics in a game.

BOOKS

Flynn, Brendan. *The NBA Encyclopedia for Kids*. Minneapolis, MN: Abdo Publishing, 2022.

Mahoney, Brian. *GOATs of Basketball*. Minneapolis, MN: Abdo Publishing, 2022.

Ybarra, Andres. *Great Basketball Debates*. Minneapolis, MN: Abdo Publishing, 2019.

ONLINE RESOURCES

To learn more about the Sacramento Kings, please visit **abdobooklinks.com** or scan this QR code. These links are routinely monitored and updated to provide the most current information available.

INDEX

Adelman, Rick, 8, 18, 20, 31
Archibald, Nate "Tiny," 17, 29–30
Bibby, Mike, 7–8, 11, 18, 31–32
Bryant, Kobe, 5, 7–9, 11

Chamberlain, Wilt, 26
Christie, Doug, 18
Cousins, DeMarcus, 20, 32–33
Cousy, Bob, 26, 29

Davies, Bob, 13, 25, 26
Divac, Vlade, 8, 11, 18, 31
Donaghy, Tim, 11

Evans, Tyreke, 20, 33

Fitzsimmons, Cotton, 37
Fox, De'Aaron, 33

Harrison, Jack, 13
Harrison, Lester, 13, 14, 25–26
Horry, Robert, 11

Jackson, Bobby, 9
Jackson, Phil, 5, 6, 9
Johnson, Kevin, 41

Lacey, Sam, 30
Lucas, Jerry, 28

Maloof family, 20, 41

O'Neal, Shaquille, 5, 11, 39

Petrie, Geoff, 7, 18, 20, 30–31

Ranadivé, Vivek, 23, 41
Richmond, Mitch, 30, 39
Risen, Arnie, 14, 26, 35
Robertson, Oscar, 15–16, 28–29, 33

Sabonis, Domantas, 33
Stern, David, 11
Stojaković, Peja, 18, 31
Stokes, Maurice, 35–37

Thacker, Tom, 28
Türkoğlu, Hedo, 18
Twyman, Jack, 15, 26–27, 37

Wanzer, Bobby, 25–26
Webber, Chris, 8, 18, 20, 30–31
Williams, Jason, 31–32
Wilson, George, 28

ABOUT THE AUTHOR

David J. Clarke is a freelance writer. Originally from Helena, Montana, he now lives in Savannah, Georgia, with his golden retriever, Gus.